This book contains
TWO
Circuit Assembly Program Notebooks for Kids!

Date:_____

Date:_____

Name:_____Age:_____

Congregation:_____

City:_____

ISBN:9781941775608

Circuit Assembly of Jehovah's Witnesses

Don't Give Up

In Fulfilling the Law of CHRIST!

Name: _____

Congregation: _____

Date: _____

20___-20___

C_rc__t

As___mb___

Pr_g__

With

Br____h

R_pr___entat_v_

Who is visting?_____

MORNING

What time should I be in my chair before the program?

MUSIC

starts at ___:___ am

 SONG NO. _____

WHO are you sitting with?

_____

_____

10:00

Wh__ I_ T___ L__ o_ C_____

SCRIPTURES

_____
_____
_____
_____
_____

count how many times you hear:

Law _____
Christ _____
Jehovah _____
Bible _____

unscramble ✱✱✱✱ ↓↓↓↓↓

WLA _____
HRCIST _____
HVEJOHA _____

```
N  T  S  O  V  B  Q  M  A  F
B  S  A  Z  P  J  H  M  U  D
B  I  R  G  P  R  A  Y  E  R
Z  R  N  I  A  F  U  A  U  H
M  H  N  C  W  D  M  P  P  Q
M  C  S  S  R  A  G  B  E  F
B  T  O  J  E  H  O  V  A  H
P  F  U  L  F  I  L  L  A  W
I  U  C  L  E  V  I  G  B  B
C  Z  F  D  O  G  T  N  O  D
```

Christ
Dont
Fulfill
Give
God
Jehovah
Law
Prayer
Up

Galashans _____ 6:2

correct the spelling ↱

"Go on the _____

of _____ another, _____

and _____ this _____

You will _____

the _____ of

"

_____ .

What is the law of Christ?

HOW do I show my love for the brothers and sisters in my congregation?

Draw a picture
↓ ↓ ↓

10:15

F_____

the I____ of

C_____ W_____

U_____ B_

H_____

Define UNSEEN_____

_____

(unscramble) NAHMUS_____

SCRIPTURES _____

_____

_____

NOTES

_____

_____

_____

_____

_____

_____

True or False: Jehovah can see me EVERY DAY of my life. _____

unscramble

SNUENE _____

Start

End ☺

Draw a picture!

1 Corinthians 10:31

"Therefore, whether you are _____ or _____ or doing anything _____, do _____ things for _____'s _____."

10:30

Fu_fi___i__ t_e L__ o_ C_ri__ i_ t__ Fi___d M_n__tr_

HOW OFTEN DO YOU GO IN THE FIELD MINISTRY?

My goal is to get ____ hours in the field ministry next month!

My favorite publication to use in the ministry is _____.

SCRIPTURES

_____

_____

_____

NOTES

draw a pic in the ministry

WHO do you go out in the ministry with?

Luke 16:10 "The _____ _____ in what is _____ is faithful _____ in _____, and the person _____ in what is _____ is _____ also in _____."

Matthew 22:39 "The _____, _____ it, is this: 'You _____ _____ your _____ as _____."

Acts 20:35 "... you must _____ those who are _____ and must _____ in mind the words of the _____ _____, when he himself said, "There is _____ _____ in _____ than there is in _____."

WHAT are the different forms of preaching?

① _____

② _____

③ _____

Draw literature in the cart!

Have you tried cart witnessing?

_____

Who can you go cart witnessing with?

_____

I love Jehovah with my whole [____]!

What 's _____ _____

subject do we preach about?

The LO☐☐ 11:05

of C☐☐i☐t

W___ S___er___r?

What is the meaning of the word SUPERIOR?

Why is Jehovah's way of life BETTER than any other way?

_____

_____

Jehovah's only-begotten son:

___ ___ ___ ___ ___ ___ ___ ___ ___ ___ ___

WHY is the LAW of Christ SUPERIOR ?

HOW is YOUR LIFE BETTER because of Jehovah?

_____

_____

scriptures

_____

_____

_____

_____

_____

NOTES

_____

_____

_____

_____

✳ HOW many times do you hear:

✳ Jehovah _____

✳ Superior _____

✳ Christ _____

✳ Scripture _____

```
C  L  R  L  V  P  B  A  A  X
J  L  R  O  I  R  E  P  U  S
E  I  N  C  N  A  M  L  D  F
H  F  J  Y  V  V  I  P  L  J
O  L  E  T  L  C  N  L  E  G
V  U  C  J  H  U  I  R  I  O
A  F  D  R  L  Q  S  R  F  D
H  O  I  L  I  N  T  P  N  U
B  S  U  A  N  X  R  L  I  Q
T  D  Q  W  I  R  Y  J  T  U
```

Christ
Field
Fulfill
God
Jehovah
Law
Ministry
Superior

from puzzle-maker.com

11:05

DEDICATION
and
B_ _p_ _ _ _s_ _ _

Speaker: _____

What is <u>BAPTISM?</u>

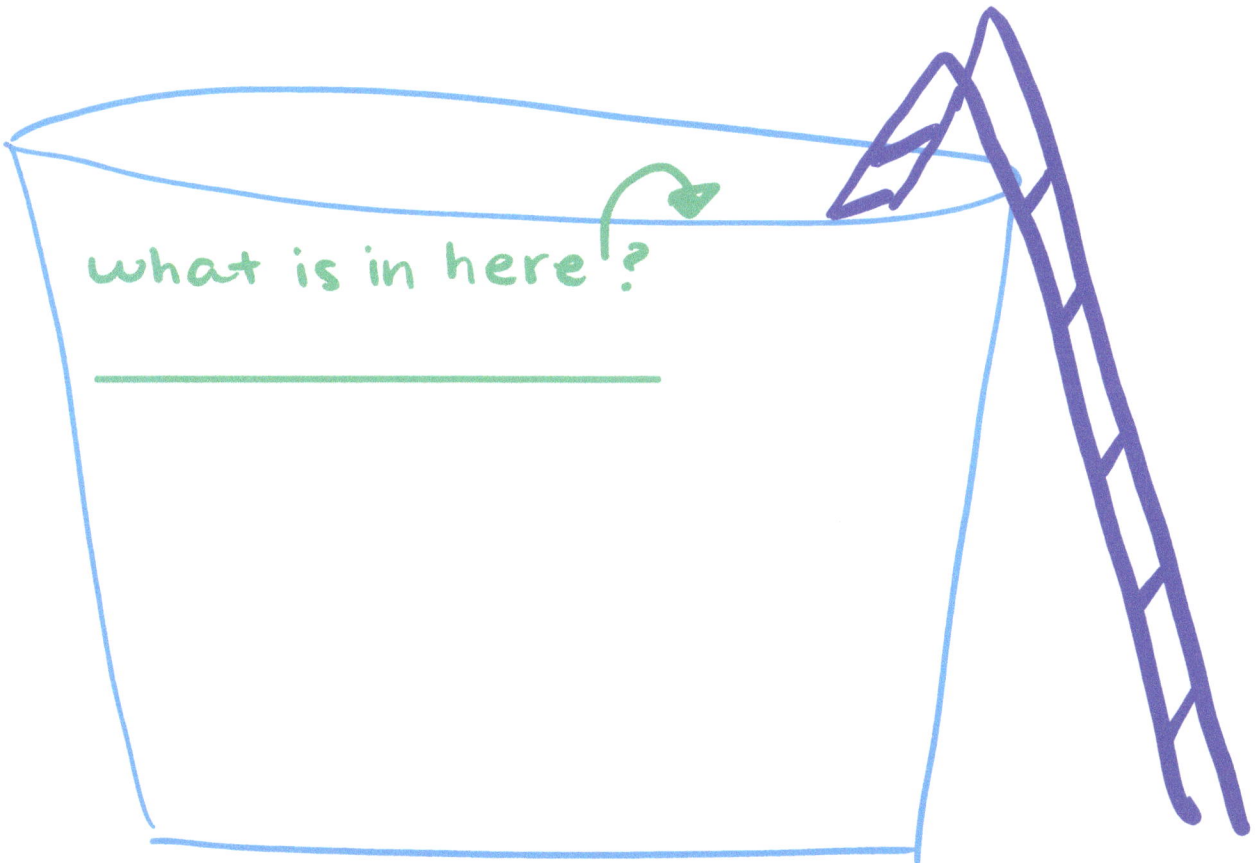

what is in here?
_____

SEARCH BAPTISM in the JW Library App (in the Bible) and write the first four scripturers:

① _____

② _____

③ _____

④ _____

Why do you think a person gets baptized?

_____

_____

_____

Scriptures   NOTES

AfteRNOON

The music starts at __:___ pm

What time should I be in my seat?

1:30 Song _____

1:35pm EX__ER__NCE_

draw a picture

What is the Theme of this Circuit Assembly?

1:45 Summary of _____

2:15pm

Ful_____li___ t_e

L_w o_ C_ri___ in the

Family

Name the members of your family:

_____

_____

Ephesians 5:23 " because a _____
is _____ of his _____ just as _____
is head of the _____..."

scriptures ☺

_____

_____

_____

_____

_____

NOTES

HOW do PARENTS fulfill the law of Christ?

HEBREWS 5:14 "But _____ food belongs to _____ people, to those who _____ use have their _____ of discernment trained to distinguish both _____ and _____."

Start

End

Ephesians 5:25 "_____,
continue _____ your _____,
just as the _____ also loved
the _____ and _____
himself _____ for it."

I LOVE MY Family!

Draw a picture of your family:

2:30
Fulfilling the _____

of _____ at

_____

Psalms 1:2 "But his _____ is in

the _____ of _____, And he _____

His _____ in an _____ day and

_____.

When I am at school, I take every
opportunity to: _____

_____

Scriptures

Do I know how to explain why I choose **not** to salute the flag?

YES

NOT YET

John 17:14 Why does the world "hate" us?

How was Jesus treated while on earth?

John 17:14

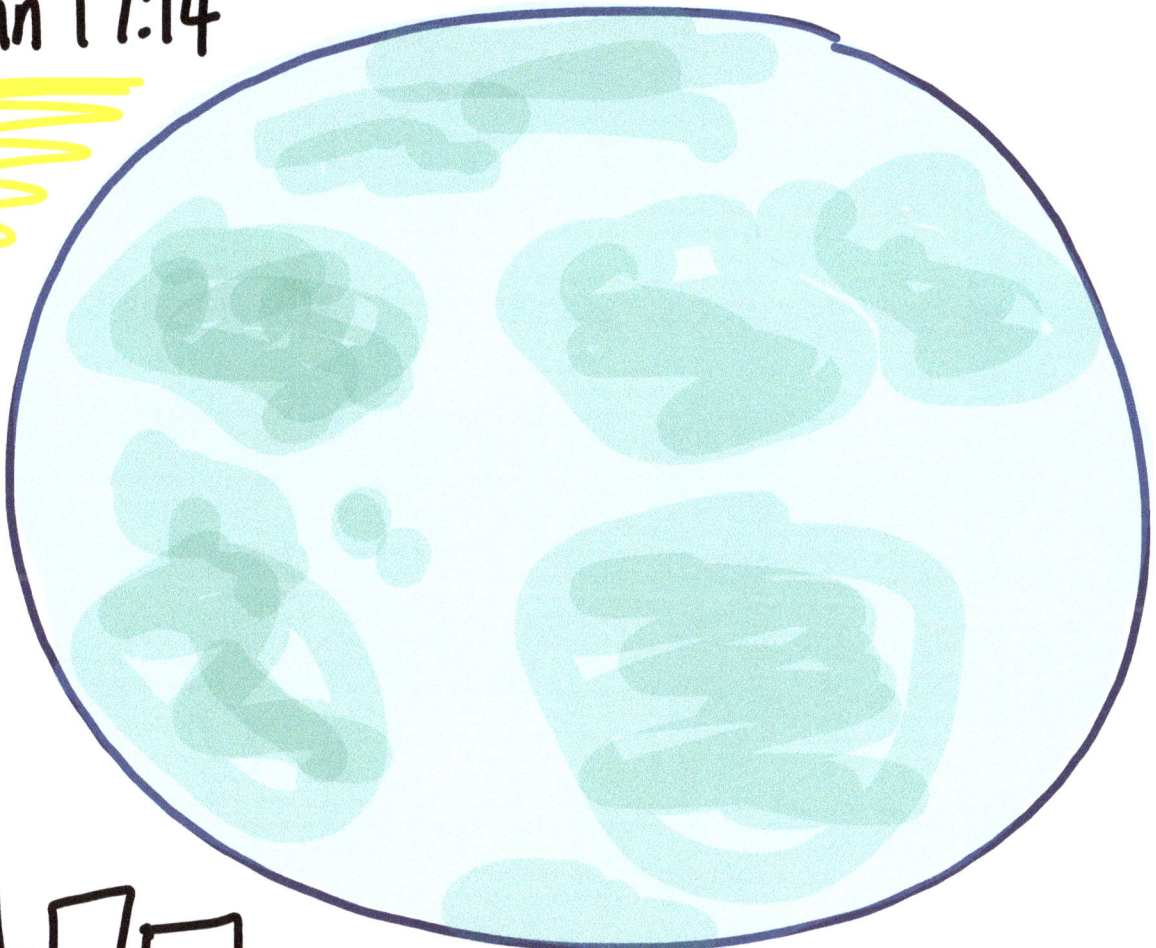

WE are
no _____
of the _____

2:55pm

Lo___ One

An___ h___,

J___ S__ A_

Je_ v__ Loved

YOU

Scriptures: _____

_____

_____

Notes: _____

_____

_____

Galatians 6:4 "But let _____ one _____ his own _____, and then he _____ have _____ for _____ in regard to _____ alone, and not in _____ with the other _____."

HOW can I love others like Jesus did?

Wo_k w_a_ is g___d tow___d a___, Galati___ 6:10 but es____cia_ly t__ard t_os_ re___t__ t_ us i_ _he _ai___.

Scripture

Galatians 6:2

1 Corinthians 10:31

Luke 16:10

1 Peter 2:16

Ephesians 5:25

Psalms 1:3

Galatians 6:10

Matching

Faithful in least is faithful in much

Fulfill the law of Christ

Do all things for God's glory

Christ loved the congregation

Be as free people, slaves of God

Work good toward ALL

He is like a tree planted by streams of water

My favorite part of today's program was:

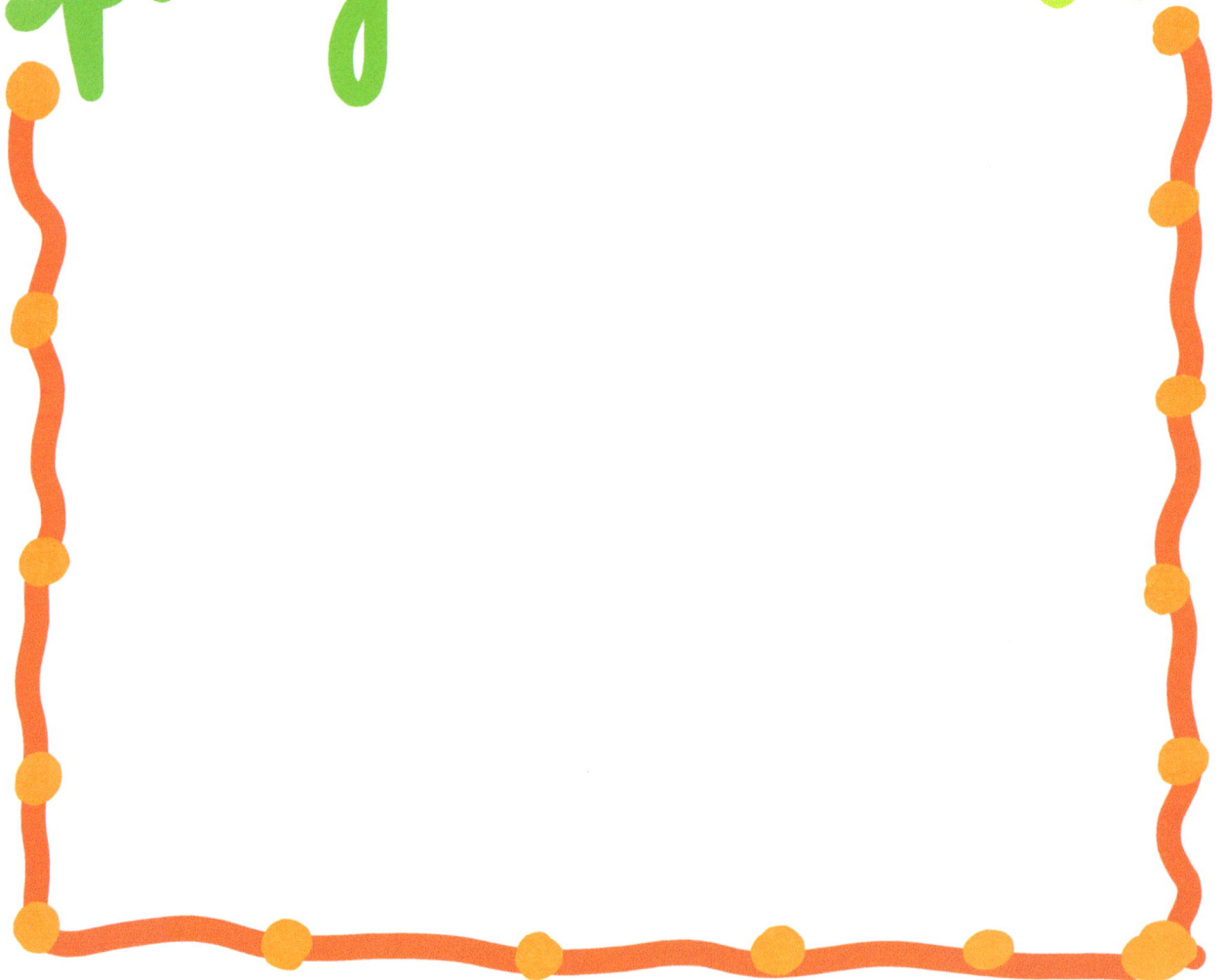

END OF PROGRAM NOTES for Don't Give Up Fulfilling the Law of Christ

Next:
Don't Give Up In Doing What Is Fine!

Don't Give Up In Doing What Is Fine!

Circuit Assembly
of
Jehovah's Witnesses
Don't Give Up
In Doing
What is Fine!

Name: _____

Congregation: _____

Date: _____

2 _ _ _ _ 1 _ _ _ - _ 0 1 _

C _ _ _ c u _ _ _

A s _ _ _ m _ l _
_ o _
J _ _ _ o _ a _ ' _ _
W _ t _ _ _ _ s e _

with

Circuit

Overseer

MORNING

the program starts at _____ : _____ am

WHO are you sitting with?

I am EXCITED

for today's program because:

I LOVE JEHOVAH

because:

I am THANKFUL for:

_____

_____

_____

SONG ___

9:50

WHY is it _____

to Do _____ is _____?

scriptures

_____
_____
_____
_____

NOTES:
_____
_____

Count the number of times you hear:

FINE _____

DON'T GIVE UP _____

DIFFICULT _____

UnsCrAMbLE:

fidfcilut _____

videl _____

wtachufl _____

dgo _____

Romans 12:2 "And _____ being _____ by this _____ of things, but be _____ by _____ your mind _____..."

WHAT warning

is given at 1 Peter 5:8?

_____

_____

_____

_____

HOW do you think Jehovah feels when you have fine behavior?

NOTES

_____

_____

_____

10:05

S_ _ mp_ _ _ i_ _ _:
A ☐ 0I ☐ So_ in_
to the _____

• Use _____ _____

Wisely

Do you use social media? _____

If so, which ones? _____

HOW can you use social media wisely?

_____

_____

_____

_____

Galatians 6:8

"because the one _____ with a view

to his _____ will reap _____

from his _____, but the one

_____ with a view to the

_____ will _____ "

_____ life from the _____.

Scriptures

Notes Notes Notes

_____

_____

_____

_____

_____

How can I use social media to praise Jehovah?

Circuit Assembly of Jehovah's Witnesses

```
E H A H J F S Q M I F R K I T
V F U N L T I S A Z T L F J V
P P I E Z O Y V R D E P E B S
R B Z K U H X X G U N L D S I
A Y L B M E S S A E R J H T H
I B W I S E L Y T W E D E X R
S Z H T C N S B S K T M G K E
E S F M I Z L H N L N E O G T
U O M O C G B Y I J I D E R T
T C J S O W I N G L I I D V I
X I K O O B E C A F R A A Y W
S A Q O R X C A V O I D M F T
L L C H L G H J E H O V A H I
P D S Y M P O S I U M P F M E
T I U C R I C X J U O L F P P
```

Assembly
Avoid
Circuit
Facebook
Flesh
Instagram
Internet
Jehovah

Media
Praise
Social
Sowing
Symposium
Twitter
Wisely

from puzzle-maker.com

Instagram @JWDOWNLOADS

_ y m _ o s _ _ _ _ _ :

Ch o o s e

W h o l e o o e

En e r t a i n m e nt

SCRIPTURES

True or False: _____
Jehovah is happy when
I choose wholesome
entertainment.

What is wholesome entertainment?

notes

_____

_____

_____

_____

_____

_____

_____

_____

What are some wholesome activities my family can do together? (Draw a pic)

Start

End 😊

Sym_____m:

F_g_t t_e S_iri_ o_ E___y

Search ENVY in the JW App
Write the first 4 scriptures in the results:

① _____

② _____

③ _____

④ _____

WHAT is ENVY?

Scriptures  NOTES

* _____
* _____
* _____
* _____

_____

_____

_____

_____

Romans 8:6 "For _____ the _____ on the _____ means _____, but _____ the _____ on the _____ means _____ and _____."

unscramble

FESLH _____

ISPRIT _____

FLEI _____

ECPAE _____

Symposium: _____

Invest in a

S _____ F _____

How can 主 invest in a secure future?

Scriptures

_____
_____
_____

What is the meaning of the word SECURE?

Describe your future thanks to Jehovah:

_____
_____

draw a picture of
your future!

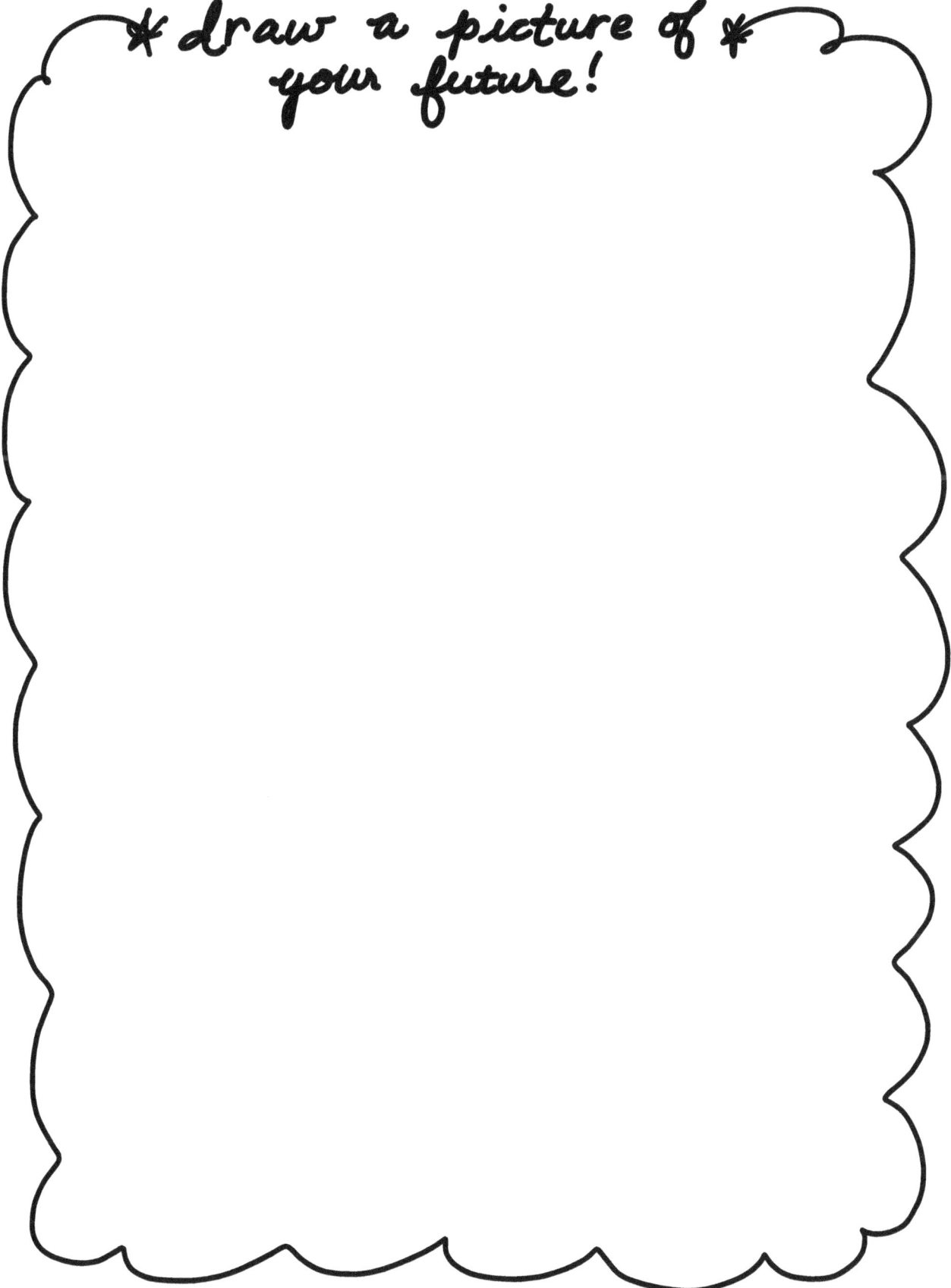

Complete the Sentence

My future will be

_____

Jehovah is

_____

I love preaching because

_____

I show Jehovah I love him by

_____

I love Jehovah with all of my

_____

11:15

KEEP W_____
GOOD

toward ___ ___ ___

Galatians 6:10

"So then, as _____ as we have the _____, let us _____ what is _____ toward _____, but _____ toward those _____ to us in the _____."

WHO are the ones "related to us in the faith"?

unscramble: **TIFAH** _____

SCRIPTURES · NOTES *

1.
2.
3.
4.
5.

HOW can I "work good toward all"?

```
V K J Z R C D R L C E          All
C E O N A E T E W F N          Faith
X F K R M N L F L Z F          Galatians
D X S N A I T A L A G          Good
R D O O G H G L T U G          Keep
A Y L U P E E K Y E A          Opportunity
W W S O Q A I X J A D          Related
O U M F A I T H E P P          Toward
T Q T B D A L L M X I          Working
P G W O R K I N G A D
O P P O R T U N I T Y
```

11:30

De☐☐i☐a☐io☐

and

Ba☐☐t☐☐m

Who do you know that is baptized?

_____

_____

_____

Think of a spiritual word that starts with each letter:

D _____

E _____

D _____

I _____

C _____

A _____

T _____

I _____

O _____

N _____

draw a picture of someone getting **Baptized!**

Afternoon!

My favorite part of the MORNING session was:

Instagram @JWDOWNLOADS

1:30

P _ _ _ _ _ _ _
Di _ _ c _ _ ur _ _

Bible

AVOID

GOD = IN WH_ _ SE_S_?

HOW
can someone
"mock God"?

_ _ _ _ _ _
_ _ _ _ _ _
_ _ _ _ _ _

SCRIPTURES

1 _____

2 _____

3 _____

4 _____

5 _____

Correct the spelling of the following words:

DISKOURSE

PUBLIK

SENCE

JEHOVA

FIINE

FUTUR

DEDECATION

WURKING

SOCUAL MEDEA

BAPTICM

STUDEE

NOTES

Watchtower Summary

MY comment:

paragraph _____

_____

_____

_____

_____

draw a picture related to the study

2:40 S_m_ _o_ _i_ _m:

K_ _ _ _ S_ _ _ _ _ _

to the

Develop G_____

S_____ H_____

SCRIPTURES

HOW CAN I IMPROVE MY STUDY HABITS?

According to Galatians 6:8, what is the reward for sowing with a view to the spirit? _____

_____

_____

What will happen to those who are sowing with a view to the FLESH? _____

_____

Notes

_____

_____

_____

_____

_____

_____

True or False:

I should be reading the Bible at least 1 time EVERY DAY!

_____

am I reading the Bible daily?

YES   NOT YET

Symposium: _____

U se B___ P_____
to G___ Y_ L__

Which Bible Principles are mentioned in the talk?

① _____

② _____

PICTURE!

scriptures

_____

_____

_____

_____

_____

HOW am I showing Jehovah that (Bible) principles guide My Life? ☺

WHO are good examples of people who use Bible principles to guide their life?

① _____

② _____

③ _____

Symposium: _____

"Do  Let

 Hand _____

↳Trace your hand here!↲

```
Y  V  T  B  X  O  X  R  G  M  T  J  O
A  U  D  I  H  W  B  J  B  E  I  E  X
D  I  R  B  Q  B  E  B  K  N  R  S  O
R  K  K  L  D  H  P  E  W  I  I  U  U
Y  Z  R  E  O  P  G  S  E  F  P  S  Y
R  F  D  V  T  Q  Y  R  K  C  S  T  A
Z  H  A  S  Y  F  Y  U  L  S  Z  X  S
A  H  E  T  O  A  A  O  C  T  D  V  T
S  R  E  O  U  L  B  C  H  E  I  H  U
E  V  H  N  R  C  P  S  A  F  X  A  D
J  H  I  N  A  I  M  I  P  X  D  N  Y
S  O  W  I  N  G  U  D  P  O  K  D  R
Y  L  I  M  A  F  S  B  Y  C  B  N  E
```

Bible	Jesus
Discourse	Not
Family	Rest
Fine	Sowing
Hand	Spirit
Happy	Study
Jehovah	Your

scriptures

notes ♥

draw a picture!

3:40pm What

WE will _____

if WE do _____

T☐R☐ — — — — —

Galatians 6:9 " So _____ us _____

_____ up in _____

what is _____, for in due _____

we will _____ if we do _____

_____ out. "

WHAT is the meaning of the word

REAP?

SCRIPTURES:

NOTES

My Favorite part of today's program:

www.ingramcontent.com/pod-product-compliance
Lightning Source LLC
Chambersburg PA
CBHW041434040426
42452CB00023B/2978